I AM SAFE

A Child's Book of Personal Safety

Written by Kate Soucheray

Illustrated by Margaret Soucheray

Wakefield Editions
PO Box 30
Westminster, MD 21158
1993

Published by *Wakefield Editions*, a subsidiary of Christian Classics, Inc.,
P.O. Box 30, Westminster, MD 21158-0930
Tel: (410) 848-3065
Toll Free: (800) 888-3065
FAX: (410) 857-2805

ISBN 0-9634674-0-9

Library of Congress Catalog Card Number: 93-60819

Printed in the U.S.A

Dedication

For John, Maggie, Bobby and John Henry

K.W.S

For my grandparents,
Grandpa and Grandma Soucheray,
and
Grandpa and Grandma Walsh

M.K.S.

Acknowledgments

I would like to thank God for the inspiration, motivation and direction He has given me as I moved through the writing and publication of this book.

I acknowledge the friends and colleagues who have generously given advice, inspiration and encouragement:

Marcie Brooke and Peg Lindlof of Working Parent Resource Center, St. Paul, MN; Anne Bastien Petersen; Mary Walsh DeRuntz; Carole Gesme, MA, C.C.D.P.; Terry Heimerl of the Convent of the Visitation School, St. Paul, MN; Mary Rita Kurtz; Marion London of Project Charlie and Project Safe, Edina, MN; Mike and Becky McGraw; Mark and Sue McKeown; Patricia Skahan-Latteral; Debbie Soucheray; John and Maggie Soucheray; Mary Kay and Katie Sprangers; Vince and Maureen Walsh, my parents; Patty Wetterling of the Jacob Wetterling Foundation.

Special thanks to:

Mike McGraw - Hagen MicroAge Computers, Richfield, MN

LB Graphics, LTD., Minneapolis, MN

Susan McKeown - Hidden picture pages, St. Paul, MN

TABLE OF CONTENTS

Introduction

Childhood is a time of creativity, imagination and freedom. Some may say that introducing our children to safety issues at an early age may make them wary of people and the wonder of life. An attitude like this can leave our children defenseless though, just what we don't want.

It's almost impossible for us as parents and care givers to think of others hurting our children. However, we read stories every week of attempted child abductions or of children who have been sexually abused. We may feel helpless. We want to know what we can do. Healthy lives for our children will come, fostered in an environment of safety. We know they will grow strong and wise and well through our guidance. We are not always with them, however, to help protect them from situations that may cause them danger. It is then that we must rely on them to know what to do to help protect themselves.

How can small children defend themselves? With the tools we give them, they will have a better chance of knowing what to do and what to say if a threatening or scary situation should arise.

This is a book written with love. It is written for us, the adults, as much as it is for the children. If we are to have the confidence to know our children can protect themselves, what we read to them must convey that message. This book does that.

It is a simple book that empowers and affirms the abilities of children to protect themselves in potentially difficult situations. It's meant to be read in a relaxed and comfortable atmosphere.

There are several instances that recommend role playing, giving the children an opportunity to practice saying the words that will help them be safe. Activity pages follow each chapter to allow children to practice what they've just learned.

There are many signs to look for if you suspect that a child has been, or is being, sexually abused. These signs can also be indicators of other possible problems, so don't assume that these signs will always mean that abuse has occurred. Follow your instincts. If you suspect sexual abuse, seek professional help. If a child has told you of abuse, affirm the child and see that they are safe. Report this information to your local Child Protection Agency or your local Law Enforcement Office.

It's very important that our children know they can tell us anything and that we will listen to them. To a child being abused, the fear of having no one to tell, or of not being believed, may be as frightening and as damaging as the abuse itself.

It has been proven that children rarely lie or make up stories about abuse.

Where there is one child being abused, it's very possible there are others. In order to protect all of our children, we must listen to them when they trust us to help them.

Our goal as care giver is to raise healthy, happy children. One of the most important foundations we can give them is the feeling of safety. If, in spite of our best efforts, something happens to them, we must show them through our swift and confident actions, that we will do all we can to restore them to safety and security.

Chapter 1

Hi! We'd like to talk to you about safety.

Safety is very important. Children feel safer when they know the rules for safety. You probably already know many of them.

One of them is to always hold the hand of a grown-up whenever you cross the street. If you're old enough to cross by yourself, you know you must always look both ways first.

Another important rule is to always buckle your seat belt whenever you ride in a car.

Be sure you ask your parents or day care person before you go to a friend's house, the park or any other place out of your yard. Always let them know where you are.

If you're away from your home with your parents or another person or group, always let them know where you are. Never leave without telling them where you are going.

There are other important ways for you to be safe. One of them is to keep your body safe.

We all have private parts of our bodies. A private body part is anything covered by a bathing suit.

For girls, these private body parts are her breasts, vagina, anus and buttocks.

For boys, these private body parts are his penis, testicles, anus and buttocks.

These private body parts are very special. They are so special that the only one who has the right to touch them is you.

Moms and dads should talk to you about why they need to touch your private body parts.

Your doctor should also talk to you about why they need to touch your private body parts.

Can you think of some times when your moms or dads or doctors would need to touch your private body parts?

Private body parts are very special. Can you think of something that is very special to you? Do you have a favorite doll, toy or book? Do you have a favorite blanket or stuffed animal you sleep with at night?

How would you feel if someone came to your house and played with this special thing without asking your permission first? How would you feel if they took it and left?

You have the right to take care of your special, private body parts just as you would take care of a special toy, blanket or stuffed animal.

Sometime, if someone you know or someone you don't know, asked to look at your private body parts, tell them "NO!" Leave that person and go to an adult you trust and tell them what happened.

Do you know what it means to trust someone? It means you believe in a person and that you think they will help you.

Who are some people you trust? Are they your parents or teachers? Are they a relative or neighbor?

Sometime, if someone you know or someone you don't know, wanted to touch your private body parts, tell them "NO!" Leave that person and go to an adult you trust and tell them what happened.

Sometime, if someone you know or someone you don't know, wanted to show you their private body parts, tell them "NO!" Leave that person and go to an adult you trust and tell them what happened.

Sometime, if someone you know or someone you don't know, wanted you to touch their private body parts, tell them "NO!" Leave that person and go to an adult you trust and tell them what happened.

If someone ever wanted to see or touch your private body parts or wanted to show you theirs or have you touch them, tell them "NO!" Leave that person and go to an adult you trust and tell them what happened.

Something like this is never to be a secret, no matter what anyone tells you. No matter what anyone tells you about keeping a secret like this, you must always tell an adult you trust.

Keeping our bodies safe is very important. Remember that you can say "NO!" to any touch that makes you feel uncomfortable.

Chapter 1, Activity 1

Scrambled Words

Unscramble the following safety words:

SAFETY PERMISSION PRIVATE BODY PARTS DOCTORS BATHING SUIT SPECIAL TOUCH LOOK TRUST TELL ADULT SECRET

1.) LELT = ____________________

2.) STURT= ____________________

3.) PAIECLS= ____________________

4.) YTEFAS= ____________________

5.) UTCHO= ____________________

6.) SORDCOT= ____________________

7.) ESTECR= ____________________

8.) GTBINAH TISU= ____________________

9.) RMOSESINIP= ____________________

10.) VTPIARE YODB RSTPA= ____________________

11.) OOKL= ____________________

12.) TULDA= ____________________

Chapter 1, Activity 2

Answer the clues first, then use the number codes to answer the question below.

1.) __ __ __ __ __ __ __ __ __ __ = Always ask this before leaving your yard.
(1,12 — 14 — 3 — 9)

2.) __ __ __ __ __ __ __ = These are people who work to keep us well.
(10 — 2)

3.) __ __ __ __ __ __ = This is when we are free from danger.
(7 15 11)

4.) __ __ __ __ __ __ __ __ __ __ __ = This is what you wear to cover your private body parts.
(8 5 6 — 16)

5.) __ __ __ __ __ = Never _ _ _ _ _ your yard unless you ask first.
(13 4)

What part of your body is very special to you and is covered when you wear a bathing suit? __ __ __ __ __ __ __ __ __ __ __ __ __ __ __ __
1 2 3 4 5 6 7 8 9 10 11 12 13 14 15 16

Chapter 1, Activity 3

Kinds of Touch

Are these kinds of touch OK or NOT OK? If they are OK, color the box beside them green. If they are NOT OK, color the box beside them red.

1.) ☐ You give your mom and dad a big hug after they take you to the park.

2.) ☐ Someone wants you to touch their private body parts. They tell you it's OK.

3.) ☐ You and a good friend sit close to each other during a scary movie.

4.) ☐ Someone you know touches your private body parts and tells you this is your special secret and that you must tell no one.

5.) ☐ Your aunt gives you a kiss on the cheek.

6.) ☐ An older friend tells you it's OK if you touch each other's private body parts. They tell you that if you don't, you can't be friends any more.

Chapter 1, Activity 4

Kinds of Touch

Are these kinds of touch OK or NOT OK?

If they are OK, color the box beside them green. If they're NOT OK, color the box beside them red.

1.) ☐ You kiss a newborn baby's face.

2.) ☐ Someone touches your bottom and tells you it's OK.

3.) ☐ You hug your mom and dad after you go to the zoo.

4.) ☐ Someone touches your private body parts and tells you this is a secret and you must not tell anyone.

5.) ☐ You haven't seen your cousins in a long time and you run to each other and give each other big hugs.

6.) ☐ Someone wants to touch your private body parts and they tell you it will feel good.

Chapter 1, Activity 5

Are these kinds of touch OK or NOT OK? If they are OK, color the box beside them green. If they're NOT OK, color the box beside them red.

1.) ☐ An older friend comes to visit and wants to touch your private body parts.

2.) ☐ An older friend comes to visit and you sit with them to read a story.

3.) ☐ Someone wants you to touch their private body parts.

4.) ☐ You give your little brother or sister a hug. (If you don't have one, pretend you do.)

Chapter 1, Activity 6

Finish each sentence below to receive your star.

1.) Someone wants to look at your private body parts and you say ______.

2.) Someone wants to touch your private body parts and you say ______.

3.) Someone wants you to look at their private body parts and you say ____.

4.) Someone wants you to touch their private body parts and you say _____.

5.) If someone wanted to look at, or touch, your private body parts or wanted you to look at or touch theirs and they wanted you to keep this a secret, you say _______.

If you said NO! to all of the sentences, color and cut out the star. Pin it to your shirt.

I SAY NO TO TOUCHING PRIVATE BODY PARTS!!!

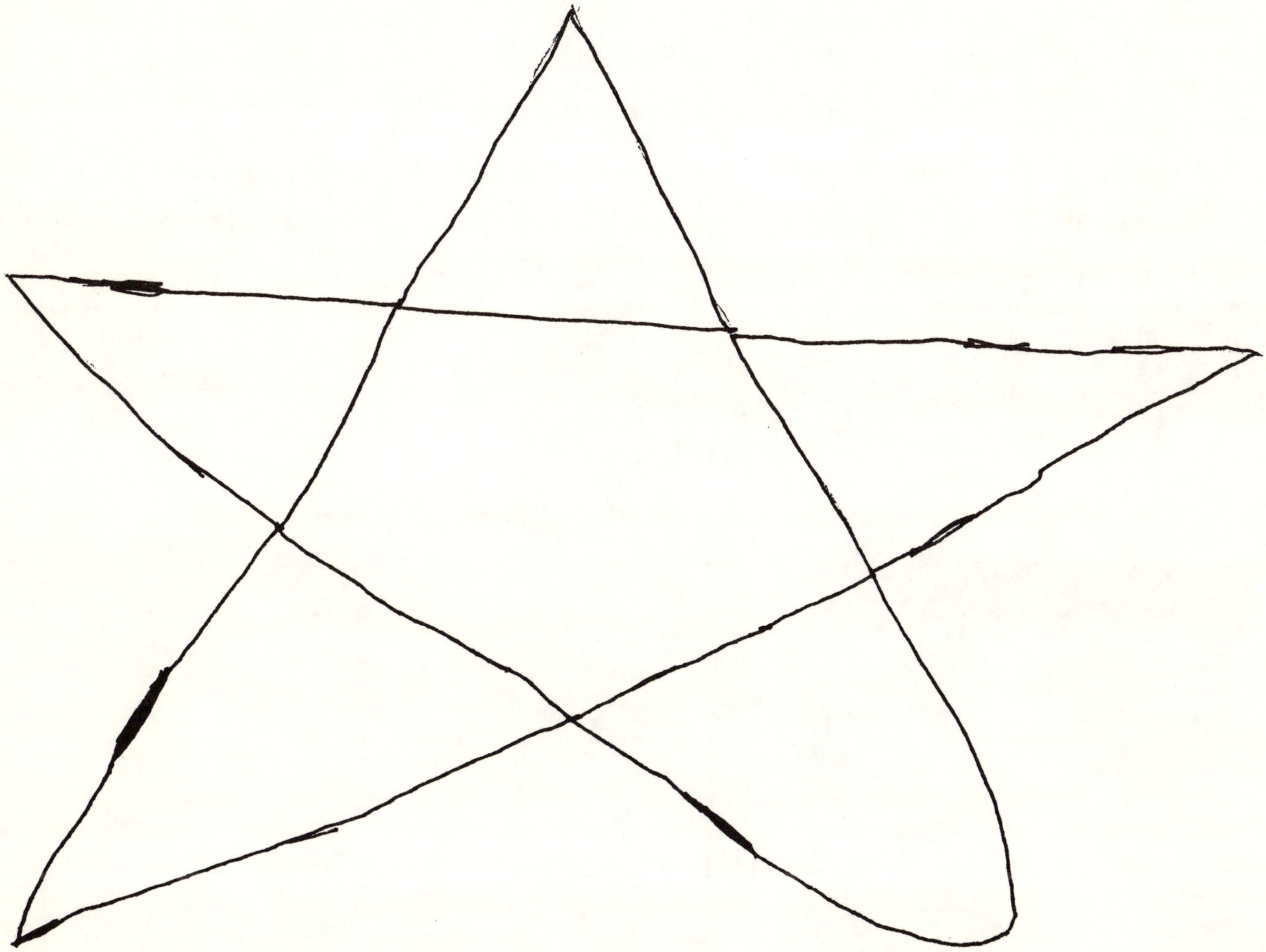

Chapter 1, Activity 7

Hidden Pictures. Find the hidden objects in the picture below:

doll, teddy bear, doctor's stethoscope, truck, baseball bat, book, pencil

Chapter 2

There is another way to be safe and that is to stay away from strangers. A stranger is someone you have not met or seen before.

Sometime you might notice a car you don't recognize near your home or play areas. It's important to stay away from any cars that are unfamiliar to you.

Sometime a stranger might ask you to come to their car or somewhere else to see a kitty or puppy. They might want to give you candy or gum. They might tell you they are lost and need help finding their way.

If anything like this ever happens to you, leave that stranger. Do not talk to strangers and do not take things from strangers.
Strangers may not be safe.

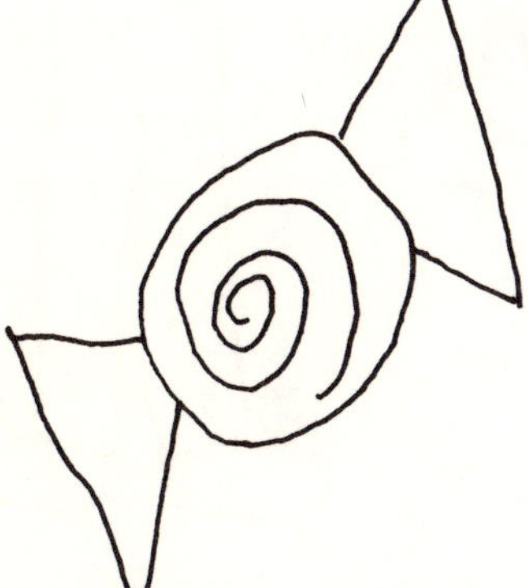

If a stranger knows your name, and you know you've never seen or met that person before, they are still a stranger. Trust yourself. That person is still a stranger.

Sometime a stranger might hear someone you know, like your parents or friends, say your name. A stranger might read it someplace. If you know you've never seen or met that person before, they are a stranger and you must stay away from them.

Go to an adult you trust and tell them what happened.

matthew
peter
David
Katie
Molly
megan

If a stranger ever wants to give you anything or take you anywhere, tell them "NO!" Leave that stranger and go to an adult you trust and tell them what happened.

Before going anywhere with anyone -- even someone you know -- always ask your parents or day care person first. Never go with anyone unless they say it is OK.

Chapter 2, Activity 1

Scrambled Words

Unscramble the following words:

SAFE STRANGERS CARS KITTY PUPPY CANDY GUM RUN AWAY PERMISSION

1.) RRTGSEASN= ____________________

2.) RCSA= ____________________

3.) TKTYI= ____________________

4.) UPYPP= ____________________

5.) AEFS= ____________________

6.) DANCY= ____________________

7.) MGU= ____________________

8.) SIMEPRONIS= ____________________

9.) YAWA NRU= ____________________

Chapter 2, Activity 2

First answer the clues, then use the number codes to fill in the blank below

1.) __ __ __ __ __ __ = a little cat
(5 under the 3rd blank)

2.) __ __ __ __ __ __ = a little dog
(6 under the 5th blank)

3.) __ __ __ = an automobile
(2 under the 2nd blank)

4.) __ __ __ __ __ __ __ __ = someone you don't know and have never seen before.
(4 under the 7th blank)

5.) __ __ __ __ = I AM _________ is the name of this book.
(1 under the 1st blank, 3 under the 3rd blank)

__ __ __ __ __ __ is when you are free from danger.
1 2 3 4 5 6

Chapter 2, Activity 3

Hidden Pictures. Find these things hidden in the picture below:

kitty, puppy, gum, candy, car

Chapter 2, Activity 4

Are these situations SAFE or UNSAFE? If they are SAFE, color the box beside them green. If they are UNSAFE, color the box beside them red.

1.) ☐ A stranger in a car stops to ask you directions and you stay away from their car.

2.) ☐ A stranger in a car stops to ask you directions and you go to their car to talk to them.

3.) ☐ A stranger offers you candy and you say "NO!" and run away and tell an adult you trust.

4.) ☐ A stranger offers you candy and you take it.

5.) ☐ A stranger wants to show you a kitty or puppy and you say "NO!" and run away and tell an adult you trust.

6.) ☐ A stranger wants to show you a kitty or puppy and you go with them.

7.) ☐ Someone you know asks you to go with them and you say you must ask first.

8.) ☐ Someone you know asks you to go with them and you leave with them without asking first.

Chapter 2, Activity 5

Finish each sentence to receive your star.

1.) A stranger offers you candy or gum and you say ______.

2.) A stranger wants to ask you directions and you say _______.

3.) A stranger wants to show you a kitty or puppy and you say ______.

4.) A stranger knows your name and says they want to talk to you and you say _______.

5.) A stranger wants you to go with them and you say _______.

If you said "NO!" to finish each sentence, color the star and cut it out. Pin it to your shirt.

I SAY NO TO STRANGERS!!!

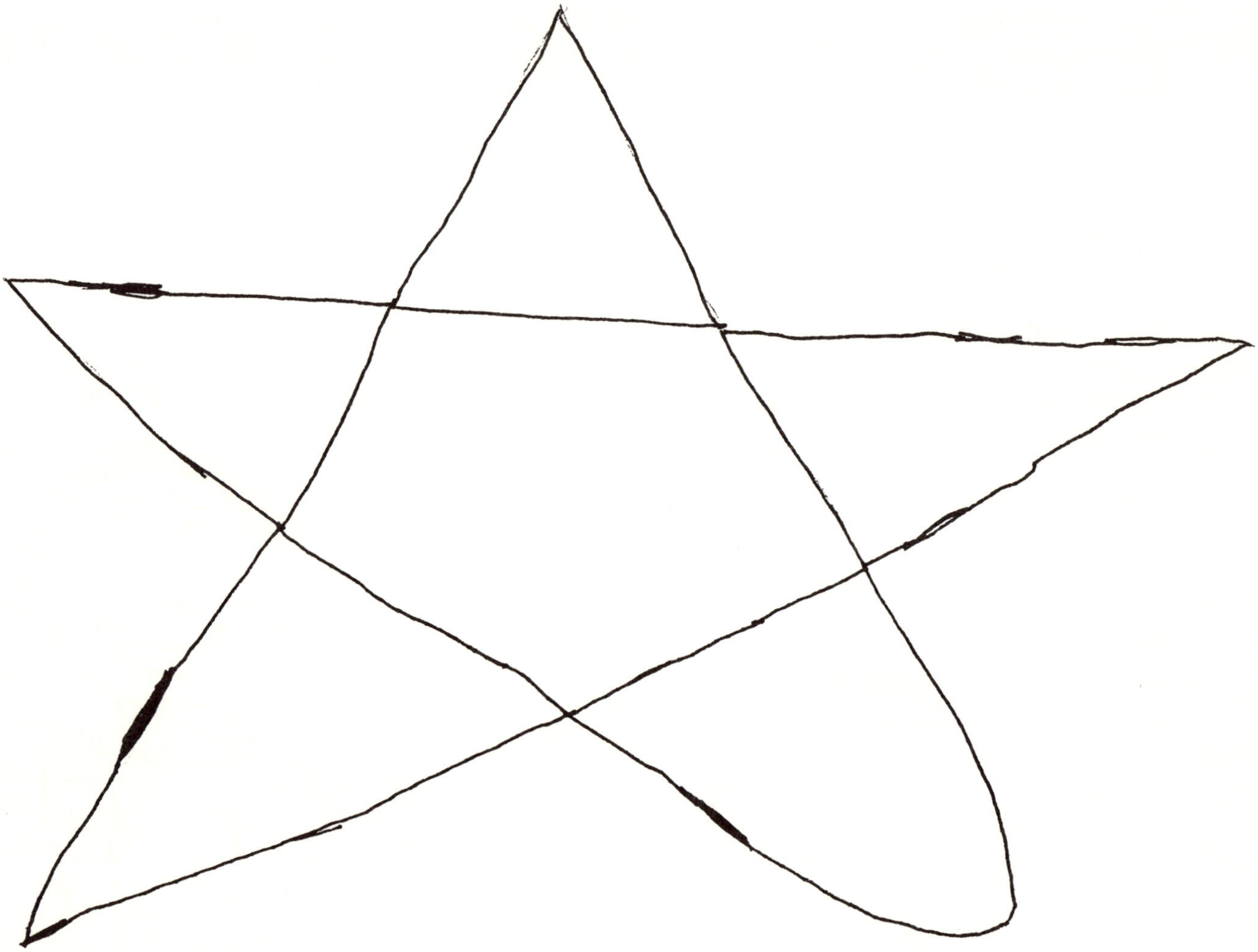

Chapter 3

Now let's talk about what to do if you get separated from your parents or person responsible for you when you're shopping or someplace else special.

Do you know what it means to get separated from someone? It means you have lost each other.

If you're shopping at a store and you get separated from the adult who brought you, you might feel like crying or yelling for them.

You might even think you should leave the store to look for them.

Whatever you feel like doing,

ALWAYS STAY IN THE STORE!!!

This is what you should do:

1.) Go to a clerk. They usually wear a name tag pinned to the front of their shirt or uniform.

2.) Tell them you are lost. Even if you're crying, they will understand you. This happens every day!

3.) Tell them your name and tell them the name of the person who brought you to the store.

4.) The clerk will call that person on a microphone that will be heard all over the store. They will come and get you.

If you're at a park, an airport, a special show or game or any other big and unfamiliar place and you get separated from your parents or the person who brought you, this is what you should do:

1.) Look for a person in a uniform. Here are what some different uniforms look like:

2.) If you don't see a person in a uniform, stay where you are.

3.) Never go with anyone you don't know or anyone not in a uniform.

4.) Cry! When people ask you why you are crying, tell them you're lost. Ask them to bring you someone in a uniform to help you. Tell them you are not to go anywhere with strangers.

5.) Your parents or person responsible for you will be looking for you. They will be calling for you and asking people if they have seen you.

6.) People will help you get together.

If a person in a uniform comes to help you, they will take you to a special place that has a microphone so that they can call your parents or person responsible for you. Remember to tell them your name and the name of the person who brought you. The person in a uniform will call them on the microphone and they will come and get you.

If you're on a field trip and you get separated from your group, do the things we just talked about.

1.) Look for a person in a uniform. If you don't see one, stay where you are.

2.) If people ask you what's wrong, tell them you're lost. Ask them to bring you someone in a uniform to help you. Tell them you are never to go anywhere with strangers.

3.) Your teacher or group leader will be looking for you.

4.) People will help to get you together.

5.) If a person in a uniform comes to help you, they will take you to a special place that has a microphone so they can call your teacher or group leader. Remember to tell them your name, the name of your school and the name of your teacher. Either your teacher or group leader will come to get you.

If you're in a woods and you get lost, you might think you should walk around and try to find your way out. It's important that you stay where you are so the people looking for you can find you.

This is what you should do:

Put your arms around a tree and stay where you are!!

People will be looking for you and calling your name. When you hear someone call your name, answer back to them. Say, "Here I Am!!!!"

Chapter 3, Activity 1

Matching uniforms.
Draw a line from the name of the person to the kind of uniform they wear.

1.) Zoo Keeper

2.) Store Clerk

3.) Police Man or Woman

4.) Airport person

(Flight Attendant or Counter person)

5.) Movie Theater Person

Chapter 3, Activity 2

Color the uniforms.

Chapter 3, Activity 3

Are these examples OK or NOT OK to do if you become separated from the person responsible for you when you're away from home? Color the box beside each example green if they're OK. Color the box beside the example red if they're NOT OK.

1.) ☐ If you get separated when you're shopping at a store, always stay in the store.

2.) ☐ If you get separated when you're shopping at a store, leave the store to look for person who brought you.

3.) ☐ If you get separated from the person who brought you to the fair, walk around and look for them.

4.) ☐ If you get separated from the person who brought you to the fair, stay where you are. Cry! When people ask you what's wrong, tell them you're lost and you need help. Ask them to bring you someone in a uniform. Tell them you never go anywhere with strangers.

5.) ☐ If you get separated from your group on a field trip, walk around and look for them .

6.) ☐ If you get separated from your group on a field trip, stay where you are. Cry! When people ask you what's wrong, tell them you're lost and you need help. Ask them to bring you someone in a uniform. Tell them you are never to go with strangers.

7.) ☐ If you're ever lost in the woods, walk around and look for a way out.

8.) ☐ If you're ever lost in a woods, put your arms around a tree and stay where you are.

Chapter 3, Activity 4

If you ever get separated from your parents or person who brought you to a store, you must always *stay in the store.*

Go to a clerk and tell them you are lost. They will call your parents or person who brought you on a microphone and they will come and get you.

A clerk usually wears a name tag. It will be pinned to the front of their uniform or shirt. It will look something like this.

Color this name tag.

Chapter 3, Activity 5

Unscramble the words below:

SEPARATED LOST STORE CRY NAME TAG CLERK
MICROPHONE UNIFORM FIELD TRIP UNFAMILIAR

1.) TSOL=____

2.) YCR= ____

3.) ELIDF PTIR= __________________________________

4.) AMNE GTA=___________________________________

5.) CPEOORINMH= ________________________________

6.) DEETRAAPS= __________________________________

7.) NFRMOIU= ___________________________________

8.) CKRLE= ______________________________________

9.) TROES= ______________________________________

10.) NMFLRUAAII= _________________________________

Chapter 3, Activity 6

First answer the clues, then use the number code to answer the question below.

1.) __ __ __ = to have tears
    13 4

2.) __ __ __ __ __ __ __ __ __ = to be lost
1,10 11

3.) __ __ __ __ __ __ __ = a special suit of clothing a person wears when they work someplace
5 12

4.) __ __ __ __ __ = a person at a check out counter in a store

5.) __ __ __ __   __ __ __ = a pin a clerk wears on the front of their uniform to tell you their name
6 3 9 7, 2

6.) __ __ __ __ = what you ask for if you become separated from your parents or the person responsible for you when you are away from home.
8 14

What must you always do if you become separated from the person who brought you to a store?

__ __ __ __   __ __   __ __ __   __ __ __ __ __
1 2 3 4   5 6   7 8 9   10 11 12 13 14

These are some important things for you to know.

Your name = ____

Your mom's name = ____

Your dad's name = ____

Your day care giver's name = _________________________________
(If you go to day care)

Your teacher's name = ______________________________________

Your address = ____

Your phone number = _(   )_______________________________

The emergency phone number = ________________________________

It's important for children to know the rules for safety. You can help keep yourself safe. Remember that you can say "NO!" to any touch that feels uncomfortable. Tell an adult you trust if anyone wants to look at or touch your private body parts or wants you to look at or touch theirs.
Tell an adult you trust if a stranger offers you candy or gum or asks you to go with them in their car.
If you ever get lost, remember to go only with people in uniforms.
Learn your address and phone number and your parent's names.

Be like us and know the rules for safety. You'll feel safer too!

Role-playing suggestions

More learning takes place when we are able to practice what we've learned. The following role-playing suggestions are easy and fun. Choose the ones you feel are appropriate for you and your children.

Chapter 1

1.) Suggest to the child that you role-play saying "NO!" to anyone who wanted to look at or touch their private body parts. Ask them, "What do you say if someone ever asked to look at or touch your private body parts?" Encourage them to say "NO!" loud and clear. Ask them what they would do if anything like this ever happened. (They should tell you they would tell an adult they trust.)

2.) Make a list with the child of whom they feel they can trust. Pretend the child needs to tell an adult they trust about someone who wanted to touch their private body parts. Role-play that situation with the child.

Chapter 2

1.) Role-play with the child what they would do if a stranger offered them candy or gum. Role-play with them what they would do if a stranger offered to show them a kitty or puppy. Role-play with them telling an adult they trust about this.

2.) Role-play with the child what they would do if someone they know asked them to go somewhere with them. Remind them that they are to always ask first.

Chapter 3

1.) Role-play with the child what they are to do if they are separated from their parents or someone else when they are shopping. It is

recommended that a family practice this at a store familiar to them, at a quiet time. Go to the store and tell the clerk what you are doing. Let the child practice “getting lost” and have them go to the clerk for help. Have the clerk call you on the microphone and show the child that you will hear this and come and get them. Praise them for staying in the store and getting help from the clerk.

2.) Whenever you go to a special game, movie or park, review with the child what they should do if you get separated. Remind them to look for someone in a uniform. Look for such a person together so that your child will recognize them if they need to later. Remind them to never go with strangers. If they are separated, remind them to tell anyone who wants to help them to bring them someone in a uniform. They are never to go anywhere with strangers.

3.) Review the child’s address and phone number (don’t forget area code).

4.) Role-play with the child how to use 911, the emergency phone number. Use a disconnected phone and practice dialing 911. The adult should play the dispatcher. The child should phone in a pretend emergency. As the dispatcher, ask the child what the problem is, what their name is and their address.

5.) Tell your child that if they are ever taken from your home by a stranger, or anyone else, they can go to any phone and dial 911 for FREE!! They need no money. Tell them this and show them places that have phones they can use. Tell them all they have to do is pick up the receiver, dial 911 and a dispatcher will answer. All they have to say is "HELP!!" If they can say their name, so much the better.

Tell them that the location of the phone they are calling from will come up on a screen to tell the 911 dispatcher where they are. A police person will be right there to help them.

I AM SAFE is a book I wrote for my children to explain safety to them. I decided to write this book for them because I want them to feel powerful, not scared, when it comes to personal safety. I want my children to know they have some control over what happens to them. I hope you and your children enjoy the book and that your children feel safer too. I hope they are able to use what they have learned.

Kate Soucheray lives in St. Paul, Minnesota with her husband and three children. She is a consultant and teacher.

Margaret Soucheray is Kate's seven-year-old daughter. She wants to be an art teacher someday.

NOTES:

NOTES:

NOTES:

NOTES: